Ministering the Word of God

by
Fr Allen Morris

*All booklets are published thanks to the
generous support of the members of the
Catholic Truth Society*

CATHOLIC TRUTH SOCIETY
PUBLISHERS TO THE HOLY SEE

Contents

All rights reserved. First published 2015 by The Incorporated Catholic Truth Society, 40-46 Harleyford Road London SE11 5AY Tel: 020 7640 0042 Fax: 020 7640 0046. © 2015 The Incorporated Catholic Truth Society.

ISBN 978 1 78469 042 7

Extract from General Introduction:
Lectionary for Mass

Gathered by Christ's Word

Christ's word gathers the people of God as one and increases and sustains them. 'This applies above all to the liturgy of the word in the celebration of Mass: there is an inseparable union between the proclamation of the death of the Lord, the response of the people listening, and the offering through which Christ has confirmed the New Covenant in his blood. The people share in this offering by their inner intentions and the reception of the sacrament.' For 'not only when things are read "that were written for our instruction" (*Rm* 15:4), but also when the Church prays or sings or acts, the faith of those taking part is nourished and their minds are raised to God, so that they may offer him their worship as intelligent beings and receive his grace more abundantly.'

Listening and responding...

In the liturgy of the word, the congregation of the faithful still today receives from God the word of his covenant through the faith that comes by hearing. The faithful must respond to that word in the same faith so that more and more they may become the people of the New Covenant.

The people of God have a spiritual right to receive abundantly from the treasury of God's word. Its riches are presented to them through use of the Order of Readings, the homily, and pastoral efforts.

For their part, the faithful at the celebration of Mass are to listen to the word of God with an inward and outward reverence that will bring them continuous growth in the spiritual life and draw them more deeply into the mystery they celebrate.

...to Christ

As a help toward celebrating the memorial of the Lord with devotion, the faithful should be keenly aware of the one presence of Christ in both the word of God - 'it is he who speaks when the holy Scriptures are read in the Church' - and 'especially under the eucharistic elements.'

To be received and integrated into the life of Christ's faithful, the word of God demands a living faith. Hearing the word of God unceasingly proclaimed arouses that faith. The Scriptures, and above all in their liturgical proclamation, are the source of life and power. As Paul attests, the Gospel is the saving power of God for everyone who believes. Love of the Scriptures is therefore the force that renews the entire people of God. All the faithful without exception must therefore always be ready to listen gladly to God's word.

When this word is proclaimed in the Church and put into living practice, it enlightens the faithful through the working of the Holy Spirit and draws them into the entire mystery of the Lord as a reality to be lived. The word of God reverently received moves the heart and its desires toward conversion and toward a life filled with both individual and community faith, since God's word is the sustenance of the Christian life and the source of the prayer of the entire Church.

When they hear the word of God and reflect deeply on it, the faithful receive the power to respond to it actively with full faith, hope, and charity through prayer and self-giving, and not only during Mass but in their entire Christian life.

Cf. General Introduction: *Lectionary for Mass* 44-48

Liturgical Ministry: What is Liturgy? What is Ministry?

Liturgy is the public worship of the Church. It is first and foremost a participation in Christ's worship of the Father, and it is in this worship that the Church is most evidently herself.

Christ is always present in his Church, especially in her liturgical celebrations. He is present in the sacrifice of the Mass, not only in the person of his minister, "the same now offering, through the ministry of priests, who formerly offered himself on the cross", but especially under the eucharistic species. By his power he is present in the sacraments, so that when a man baptizes it is really Christ himself who baptizes. He is present in his word, since it is he himself who speaks when the holy Scriptures are read in the Church. He is present, lastly, when the Church prays and sings, for he promised: "Where two or three are gathered together in my name, there am I in the midst of them" (*Mt* 18:20).

Christ indeed always associates the Church with himself in this great work wherein God is perfectly glorified and men are sanctified. The Church is his beloved Bride who calls to her Lord, and through him offers worship to the Eternal Father.

Rightly, then, the liturgy is considered as an exercise of the priestly office of Jesus Christ. In the liturgy the sanctification of the man is signified by signs perceptible to the senses, and is effected in a way which corresponds with each of these signs; in the liturgy the whole public worship is performed by the Mystical Body of Jesus Christ, that is, by the Head and his members.

From this it follows that every liturgical celebration, because it is an action of Christ the priest and of his Body which is the Church, is a sacred action surpassing all others; no other action of the Church can equal its efficacy by the same title and to the same degree.

The liturgy is the summit toward which the activity of the Church is directed; at the same time it is the font from which all her power flows. For the aim and object of apostolic works is that all who are made sons of God by faith and baptism should come together to praise God in the midst of his Church, to take part in the sacrifice, and to eat the Lord's supper.

Sacrosanctum Concilium 7, 10

Liturgy is always something more than just what we happen to do in this place, here and now. It is always a work of the whole Church. It is most fundamentally the participation of the whole Church, the Body of Christ, in the worship offered to God the Father by God the Son, Jesus Christ. It is a work that is visible here on earth but which is, invisible to us, shared in also by saints and angels.

The ordinary forms of the Liturgy are those contained in the Church's ritual books. The most regularly celebrated are the Liturgy of the Hours and the Mass, but also included are the rites of Baptism, Confirmation, Penance, Marriage etc. (the Sacraments), the rites of Christian Funerals, and rites of Blessing.

Liturgy is always intended to be prayerful, drawing us into the prayer and worship of Jesus Christ. But not all prayer is liturgical prayer. Our private prayers - such as *lectio divina* or the Rosary, or our quiet personal prayer - have a different character. Even when they are spiritual exercises especially commended by the Church they are private prayers. Prayer of this sort helps deepen our relationship with God and helps us better live our Christian lives. However in this prayer we pray essentially as individuals who come before God in our own right, and set before him ourselves, our needs, our hopes and fears. This is the case even when we pray such forms of prayer together with others, even in church.

Liturgy always has the broader ecclesial dimension, and always it is a participation in the prayer of Christ.

For this reason the Church takes the greatest care of how the Liturgy is celebrated. The liturgical books themselves witness to the care taken with regard to the proper ordering of the rites. There is clear instruction about what is to be done, at Mass for example.[1] The roles of the ministers and the congregation as a whole are described. The approved readings and prayers are provided. There is guidance about the way symbols are used and how the church building itself is to be arranged. Nothing is left to chance! But of course the guidance has to be applied to particular celebrations in particular places and at particular times.

Ministry

Christian ministry is a sharing in the mission and ministry of Jesus Christ. It is a participation made possible by our baptism, where we are anointed with the chrism of salvation so that, united with the Church, we may remain, each of us, for ever members of Christ who is Priest, Prophet and King.

This ministry which is the duty and right of all the baptised is carried out in so many ways. Some of these are the responsibility of those called to particular ministry and ordained as deacon, priest or bishop so that they may carry out the work entrusted to them. More usually the ministry is carried out by laymen and women in the daily business of family life, at work, and as active citizens of their local, national and international communities. Whatever the differences, all Christians are called to be united in making this world holy, in witnessing to the Gospel of Jesus Christ by word and deed, and in living the love of God, especially in the service of those most in need.

Mostly Christian ministry is to be exercised in the 'world' of our towns and cities, in our places of work and in our homes - wherever it is that daily life and the mission of the Church takes us. However some part of it is also exercised in church! And of that part, which includes administration, fundraising and a variety of other works, an especially important part is liturgical ministry.

Liturgical Ministry

One of my privileges as a parish priest is introducing children to their first exercise of liturgical ministry. It is usually as they prepare to be altar servers. At the very first training session I ask them who it is that, as servers, they are there to serve. The answers are interesting, and revealing.

Often the first answer is 'God'. I tell them that although that is true, that is not the answer I am looking for.

Then someone will say that they are there to serve me! I tell them that that is also true. And that I am very grateful. But that it is not the answer I am looking for.

Then, usually, someone will give me the answer I hope for: 'We are here to serve everybody else.' And I thank them for that answer - and say that when they do that God and the priest will be very happy, because in the liturgy God and the priest also are there to serve the 'everybody else', the congregation, helping them to the full active and conscious participation in the liturgy that, through baptism, is their right and their duty.

Ministries to the Liturgy take a wide variety of forms. In the General Introduction to the Roman Missal (GIRM) there is mention of that of Bishop, Priest and Deacon, the ordained ministries; the ministry of the congregation (who are also there to serve as well as be served); acolyte and lector[2] (in practice these ministries are reserved for those preparing for ordination); altar servers, commissioned ministers of the word, psalmist, the schola or choir, cantor, sacristan, those who take up the collection, those who welcome people to the church, and Master of Ceremonies.[3] One might add to the list those responsible for the preparation of the Liturgy - for example the choosing of settings for the Liturgy's sung parts, and the decoration, even the cleaning of the church where the Liturgy will be celebrated.

Collaborative ministry

The vision of the Church is that the celebration of the Liturgy be seen as a work not only of the ordained minister (essential though that is, for example, to the celebration of Mass and some of the other sacraments) but of the gathered Church. The ministers called from the community, and called in some number according to the above list, are there to assist that community in its praying of the Liturgy.

The ministers draw on their own particular skills and ability to serve the Liturgy, to allow the beauty and dignity and pace appropriate to the Liturgy to communicate itself to the congregation, so that the community gathered may celebrate worthily and fruitfully.

Training is essential for the proper exercise of ministry. Sometimes the ministry will require that the person exercising of it will develop exceptional skills - musicians need to have a certain competency in their instrument, singers know how to use their voice, and each group has to rehearse with the other so that the congregation will be helped and not hindered by the resulting sounds. Sometimes the ministry may be less specialised, less demanding but always a ministry can be exercised well or less well. Training helps it to be exercised well.

The minimum training will include ensuring ministers know

- the coordinator for their ministry (not least so they can let someone know if they are on the rota but cannot minister that day for some reason)

- the practicalities for that day (take collectors for example: where are the baskets kept? Is there a second collection today or not? Or take readers for another example - what are the readings set for a particular day?)

- the safeguarding responsibilities involved (take ministers of hospitality for example: what are the safe places for those in wheelchairs to sit? What is the policy in case of fire or other need for emergency evacuation?)

- with which other ministers they need to coordinate their ministry (musicians and readers, for example: is the Psalm being sung or said? What is happening with the Gospel Acclamation?)

However the minimum is far from being enough. Ministers need and deserve to understand how their ministry helps to support and build up the community of the Church; why the Liturgy is important and how it helps us to mature as Christians. They need and deserve also to be thanked and encouraged and helped to bond as a particular *cadre* within the family of the parish, and not only so as better to be able to support and encourage each other in the work of being a minister - which often is costly and demanding on people's time. When people are giving as much as our ministers do, they deserve their own time for care and support.

Commissioning of Ministers

The commissioning of ministers is clearly an important moment in the life of a parish, and should take place when a sizeable portion of the parish community is able to be present.

It is better to avoid the great feasts, such as the Mass of the Lord's Supper, as these already have important focusses of their own.

For the commissioning of readers, the first Sunday of Advent might be considered. The second Sunday of Advent is kept as Bible Sunday in many denominations, and 'Openness to the Word of God' is a particular focus of the *Cycle of Prayer* for the Catholic Church in England and Wales.[4]

Alternatively the first Sunday of Lent may be suitable. The Gospel of that Sunday in Year A contains the phrase: 'Man does not live on bread alone but on every word that comes from the mouth of God.' Reading and listening to Scripture is a good spiritual practice for Lent, and commissioning of readers provides a further opportunity to promote love of Scripture in the parish more broadly.

Local circumstances will suggest whether it is better to commission all ministers at a single celebration, or at the Mass at which they will most regularly serve.

Local circumstances will also determine whether ministers are commissioned for a single year, or for longer.

At the end of their time of service it should be a matter of mutual discernment between minister and parish priest whether they are to be commissioned for a further period of service.

A Theology of the Mass

At the Mass of the Lord's Supper, the first liturgy of the Sacred Paschal Triduum, we hear the following words from St Paul - the first written account of the Eucharist, the Mass, that we possess.

> This is what I received from the Lord, and in turn passed on to you: that on the same night that he was betrayed, the Lord Jesus took some bread, and thanked God for it and broke it, and he said, 'This is my body, which is for you; do this as a memorial of me.' In the same way he took the cup after supper, and said, 'This cup is the new covenant in my blood. Whenever you drink it, do this as a memorial of me.' Until the Lord comes, therefore, every time you eat this bread and drink this cup, you are proclaiming his death.

1 Co 11:23-26

The passage reminds us of several things.

- The Mass is firmly established in the Paschal Mystery of Jesus's Passion, Death and Resurrection

- The Mass is about the gift of Jesus's body and blood, the new covenant offered to us.

- The Mass is an expression of the Tradition of the Church, handed on through the Church down the ages, and presently entrusted to us.

- Our participation in the Mass - especially in the eating and drinking of the Lord's Body and Blood - is a memorial, an active remembering, of him. And our participation means that we here and now proclaim and witness to our faith in his saving death.

The *Catechism of the Catholic Church* (CCC), quoting the Second Vatican Council's teaching on the Liturgy, puts it this way:

At the Last Supper, on the night he was betrayed, our Saviour instituted the Eucharistic sacrifice of his Body and Blood. This he did in order to perpetuate the sacrifice of the cross throughout the ages until he should come again, and so to entrust to his beloved Spouse, the Church, a memorial of his death and resurrection: a sacrament of love, a sign of unity, a bond of charity, a Paschal banquet 'in which Christ is consumed, the mind is filled with grace, and a pledge of future glory is given to us.'

CCC 1323, quoting *Sacrosanctum Concilium* 47

There is much here to note - including the language of sacrifice, of love and charity, of salvation. These are themes well worth exploring in days of recollection and formation for those who are involved in ministering at celebrations of the Mass.

But here let us note in particular the way in which the passage describes the Mass in terms of a personal work of our Saviour. He institutes the sacrament of the Sacrifice at the Last Supper in anticipation of his offering the sacrifice of himself at the Cross. He does this so that the Church may be present to and given life through that sacrament always, until he comes again. In her reception of this sacrament the Church receives, herself consumes, Christ. She is filled with grace now. And she is encouraged by the pledge of future glory even as she awaits his return in glory. For the Church, by this sacrament, Calvary and the Resurrection are not past events somehow remembered. They are present realities, re-presented to us (re-presented, not merely represented) for Christ wills it. And he wills it for our sake.

The Eucharist is 'the source and summit of the Christian life.' 'The other sacraments, and indeed all ecclesiastical ministries and works of the apostolate, are bound up with the Eucharist and are oriented toward it. For in the blessed Eucharist is contained the whole spiritual good of the Church, namely Christ himself, our Pasch.'

'The Eucharist is the efficacious sign and sublime cause of that communion in the divine life and that unity of the People of God by which the Church is kept in being. It is the culmination both of God's action sanctifying the world in Christ and of the worship men offer to Christ and through him to the Father in the Holy Spirit.'

CCC 1324, 1325

To put all this at its simplest: by the will of Jesus, the Mass is for us, and we are for the world. Pope Francis recently said:

> Jesus leaves us the Eucharist as the Church's daily remembrance of, and deeper sharing in, the event of his Passover (cf. *Lk* 22:19)… The believer is essentially 'one who remembers'.
>
> *Evangelii Gaudium*, 13

We cannot remember Jesus, not really remember him, and not be moved to mission. This is an important point made by Pope St John Paul II in his letter inaugurating the 2004-2005 Year of the Eucharist, and it concerns the authenticity of our communal sharing in the Eucharist:

> In the Eucharist our God has shown love in the extreme, overturning all those criteria of power which too often govern human relations and radically affirming the criterion of service: 'If anyone would be first, he must be last of all and servant of all' (*Mc* 9:35). It is not by chance that the Gospel of John contains no account of the institution of the Eucharist, but instead relates the 'washing of feet' (cf. *Jn* 13:1-20): by bending down to wash the feet of his disciples, Jesus explains the meaning of the Eucharist unequivocally. Saint Paul vigorously reaffirms the impropriety of a Eucharistic celebration lacking charity expressed by practical sharing with the poor (cf. 1 *Co* 11:17-22, 27-34).
>
> *Mane Nobiscum Domine*, 28

The Church uses the language of 'remembering' or of 'memorial' to describe the Eucharist and our participation in it. But it uses the language in a somewhat technical and specialised way.[5] In the ordinary way of things, 'remembering' is something that happens in our mind - the conjuring up of (often rather faded and doubtful) mental memories of some past thing.

The following story - handed on by the Jewish philosopher Martin Buber - demonstrates the power of human memory when it also becomes present reality:

> My grandfather was paralysed. One day he was asked to tell something that happened with his teacher - the great Baalschem. Then he told how the saintly Baalschem used to leap about and dance while he was at his prayers. As he went on with the story my grandfather stood up; he was so carried away that he had to show how the master had done it, and started to caper about and dance. From that moment on he was cured. That is how stories ought to be told.

> Martin Buber, quoted by Michael Mayne,
> *The Enduring Melody*
> (London: Darton, Longman, & Todd, 2006, 204-205).

The transformative power of the Eucharist however does not depend only on the enthusiasm and personal commitment of those Christians present to celebrate. Most importantly it depends on the real presence of Christ. Our

new life, gifted to us in the Eucharist, is his present gift.
We need to receive it and accept it, and let it take root in us
and draw response from us. But first and foremost, through
this ritual handed on by the Church, it is Christ himself
who is personally and really present to us. It is he who
enables our remembering and prompts our response.

The Church knows Christ to be present to us in the
Liturgy in many ways.

> Christ is always present in his Church, especially in her
> liturgical celebrations. He is present in the sacrifice of
> the Mass, not only in the person of his minister, 'the
> same now offering, through the ministry of priests, who
> formerly offered himself on the cross', but especially
> under the Eucharistic species. By his power he is present
> in the sacraments, so that when a man baptizes it is
> really Christ himself who baptizes. He is present in his
> Word, since it is he himself who speaks when the holy
> Scriptures are read in the Church. He is present, lastly,
> when the Church prays and sings, for he promised:
> 'Where two or three are gathered together in my name,
> there am I in the midst of them' (*Mt* 18:20).

Sacrosanctum Concilium 7

This is extraordinary. It is a grace of the Paschal Mystery.
It is the truth that enables all Liturgy to be the occasion of
a new personal and encounter between the risen Lord and
the community of disciples: an encounter as real as those

of which we read in the Gospels - and including in it just the same encouragement and challenge.

The presences of Christ in the various stages of the Mass

The Liturgy of the Mass helps us attend to different presences of the Lord in sequence.

The Introductory Rites engage us with the assembly of the Church in this place at this time. We see Christ present in our brothers and sisters, in the young and old, men and women, rich and poor, people of all nations. We see Christ and are gathered by him into the one Body through the ministry of the priest who presides as Christ at our assembly.

The Liturgy of the Word enables us to hear the Lord speak to our hearts and minds through Sacred Scripture proclaimed by his ministers. His words come to our own lips as we join in the proclamation of the Responsorial Psalm. The priest assists in our finding nourishment in the Word, through the breaking of the bread of the Word in the homily.

In the Eucharistic Prayer for Various Needs and Occasions we acknowledge these various presences, giving thanks to God the Father and thanks for God the Son.

You are indeed Holy and to be glorified, O God,
who love the human race

and who always walk with us on the journey of life.
Blessed indeed is your Son,
present in our midst
when we are gathered by his love
and when, as once for the disciples, so now for us,
he opens the Scriptures and breaks the bread.

The celebration of the Liturgy of the Word prepares us for
the central action of the Mass, **the Liturgy of the Eucharist**,
for the prayer of Thanksgiving in which the Sacrifice of
Jesus becomes present in the act of consecration, through
the ministry of the priest, is re-presented to the Father, and
then shared with us in Holy Communion.

Thus nourished, thus sustained, in the **Concluding
Rites** the community prays, grateful for what has been
shared with it and knowing itself newly called to be the
Body of Christ for the World.

Christ present in the Eucharistic species

Catholic theology and devotion finds a particular focus
in the presence of Christ in the Eucharistic species, the
sacramental food and drink that are his Body and Blood

The mode of Christ's presence under the Eucharistic
species is unique. It raises the Eucharist above all the
sacraments as 'the perfection of the spiritual life and
the end to which all the sacraments tend.' In the most
blessed sacrament of the Eucharist 'the body and blood,

together with the soul and divinity, of our Lord Jesus Christ and, therefore, the whole Christ is truly, really, and substantially contained.' 'This presence is called "real" - by which is not intended to exclude the other types of presence as if they could not be "real" too, but because it is presence in the fullest sense: that is to say, it is a substantial presence by which Christ, God and man, makes himself wholly and entirely present.'

It is by the conversion of the bread and wine into Christ's Body and Blood that Christ becomes present in this sacrament. The Church Fathers strongly affirmed the faith of the Church in the efficacy of the Word of Christ and of the action of the Holy Spirit to bring about this conversion. Thus St John Chrysostom declares:

> It is not man that causes the things offered to become the Body and Blood of Christ, but he who was crucified for us, Christ himself. The priest, in the role of Christ, pronounces these words, but their power and grace are God's. This is my body, he says. This word transforms the things offered.

The Council of Trent summarizes the Catholic faith by declaring: 'Because Christ our Redeemer said that it was truly his body that he was offering under the species of bread, it has always been the conviction of the Church of God, and this holy Council now declares again, that by the consecration of the bread and wine there takes place a change of the whole substance of the bread into the substance of the body of Christ our Lord and of the whole substance of the wine into the substance of his blood. This change the holy Catholic Church has fittingly and properly called transubstantiation.'

CCC 1374, 1375, 1376

Worship of the Eucharist outside of Mass

The substantial character of Christ's presence in the Eucharistic species, and the practice of reserving the sacramental food in order to be able to take Holy Communion to the sick and dying, makes it possible for the faithful to gather in Christ's Eucharistic presence for private prayer (or indeed prayer in common) outside from Mass.

A particular feature of the devotional life of the Catholic Church, this form of prayer allows for communion:

The devotion prompting the faithful to visit the blessed sacrament draws them into an ever deeper share in the Paschal Mystery and leads them to respond gratefully to the gift of him who through his humanity constantly pours divine life into the members of his Body. Abiding with Christ the Lord, they enjoy his intimate friendship and pour out their hearts before him for themselves and for those dear to them and they pray for the peace and salvation of the world. Offering their entire lives with Christ to the Father in the Holy Spirit, they derive from this sublime colloquy an increase of faith, hope, and charity. Thus they foster those right dispositions that enable them with due devotion to celebrate the memorial of the Lord and receive frequently the bread given us by the Father.

Prayer before Christ the Lord sacramentally present extends the union with Christ that the faithful have reached in communion. It renews the covenant that in turn moves them to maintain by the way they live what they have received through faith and the sacrament. They should strive to lead their whole lives in the strength of this heavenly food, as sharers in the death and resurrection of the Lord. All should be eager to do good works and to please God, so that they may seek to imbue the world with the Christian spirit and, in all things, even in the midst of human affairs, to become witnesses of Christ.

General Introduction to the *Rites for Holy Communion and worship of the Eucharist outside Mass*, 80, 81

Praying with the Scriptures outside of Mass

Prayer and worship with the Scriptures outside of Mass was encouraged at the Second Vatican Council (SC 35.5). This prayer can take many different forms - the Bible services envisaged by *Sacrosanctum Concilium*, celebrations of a Liturgy of the Word; *Lectio divina*; celebrations of the Divine Office. It helps to deepen people's knowledge and love of the Scriptures, and further to assist their participation in the Mass.

Taking things further

Bring each mode of Christ's personal presence to mind and heart, and reflect on them in prayer.

- How do the Introductory Rites help you to be ready for the 'meat' of the Mass?

- What helps and hinders your being nourished by the Liturgy of the Word?

- Which parts of the Liturgy of the Eucharist particular engage you? Are there parts that you find less notable or even neglect?

- How do the Concluding Rites help us understand the mission of the Church, a mission in which we share?

- When are there opportunities in your daily or weekly routine for times of prayer nourished by the Word of God and/or prayer before the Blessed Sacrament?

The Liturgy of the Mass as it relates to the Ministry of Reader

Having taken a broader over view of the Mass, we now look at aspects of the Mass that particularly relate to the ministry of Reader.

We will look at the Liturgy of the Word in greater detail as this is where the ministry is principally carried out. But we will also look at other things which relate to the ministry of the word, as sometimes the Reader will find help for their ministry here, and also, with their particular perspective, may be able to contribute to the parish's consideration of how the Mass is celebrated so as best to benefit from the spiritual riches it contains.

Perhaps the first thing to note is how the texts of the Mass are deeply Scriptural, often directly quoting Scripture, or at least making direct allusion to Scriptural phrases and insights. Indeed the Mass may be considered a mosaic of Scriptural texts and allusions, from its first words to its last.

Take for example the following examples from the very beginning and end of the Mass, and the invitation to Holy Communion:

Priest: In the name of the Father, and of the Son, and of the Holy Spirit.	Baptise them in the name of the Father and of the Son and of the Holy Spirit. *Mt* 28:19
The grace of our Lord Jesus Christ, and the love of God, and the communion of the Holy Spirit be with you all.	The grace of the Lord Jesus Christ, the love of God and the fellowship of the Holy Spirit be with you all. *2 Co* 13:13
The Lord be with you. **And with your spirit.**	The Lord (YHWH) be with you. *Rt* 2:4 The grace of our Lord Jesus Christ be with your spirit, my brothers. *Ga* 6:18
Behold the Lamb of God, behold him who takes away the sins of the world. Blessed are those called to the supper of the Lamb. **Lord, I am not worthy that you should enter under my roof, but only say the word and my soul shall be healed.**	John (the Baptist) said 'Look there is the lamb of God that takes away the sin of the world.' *Jn* 1:29 The centurion replied, 'Sir, I am not worthy to have you under my roof; just give the word and my servant will be cured.' *Mt* 8:8
Go in peace. **Thanks be to God.**	'Your faith has saved you; go in peace.' *Lk* 7:50 Thanks be to God for his inexpressible gift. *2 Co* 9:15

What difference does this make? At one level, not much - the words mean what the words mean, and the concepts are fairly easy to grasp even if we are not especially biblically literate (though we might be pressed to explain why Jesus could be called Lamb of God, without knowing the stories of Passover and John's Gospel). But at another level it is a profound indication of how deeply the Mass is rooted in Tradition. The form, the words themselves, is handed down to us, not to be changed at whim, but treasured as expression of the Faith of the Church handed on from the Apostles and now to be received and handed on by us and our generation. The words of those who have gone before us (which is also the inspired word of Scripture), are placed on our lips. In praying the Mass the whole assembly prays the Bible.

Greater familiarity with the Scriptures will help us to a greater appreciation for the Mass. Great appreciation for the texts of the Mass will in turn help us to better love the Scriptures. And the better we love both, the better we will minister the Word at Mass.

The Principal Parts of the Mass

Introductory Rites

The principal function of the Introductory Rites is

> to ensure that the faithful, who come together as one, establish communion and dispose themselves properly to listen to the word of God and to celebrate the Eucharist worthily. *GIRM* 46

These rites serve as spiritual exercises in repentance, thanksgiving and praise. They are like the warm-up exercises of an athlete for those coming to do the work of the Liturgy and to be joined with the prayer of the Church. Serving the whole assembly in this way, they are of particular importance to the one to whom is asked to minister the word prayerfully, faithfully and fruitfully.

Liturgy of the Word

The Liturgy of the Word is made up of a number of elements - firstly the word of God, and secondly our words in response (homily, Creed and Prayer of the Faithful). Best practice is to have one reader for each of the different readings of the word of God - on Sundays three readers - one each for the first and second readings, an ordained minister for the Gospel - and a psalmist to lead the singing of the psalm. Hearing a variety of voices helps the congregation hear the Word; it also more naturally introduces brief times of silence after each reading during which people can ponder and take to heart what has been ministered to them.

However even if a reader reads only one reading, it is as a set of texts that the word is proclaimed. There is good reason for those ministering any element of the set to be familiar with the whole set.

- On Sundays in Ordinary Time (i.e. the numbered Sundays of the Year) the most closely related passages are the First Reading, the Psalm and the Gospel. The first two will have been chosen for their relationship to the Gospel, and so - in their liturgical context - will be best understood (and thus proclaimed) in that context. The Second Reading will not have been chosen because of a relationship with those other three passages, but will have a close sequential reading with the Second Reading from the Sunday before and the Sunday after. Again, context is important.

- On Sundays in the great seasons of Advent and Christmas, of Lent and Easter, all the elements of the Liturgy of the Word are related to the Gospel and the spirit of the season.

Sometimes ministers of the Word - clergy and laity - meet to prepare together. Their reflection on the readings, and how they relate to their pastoral setting can be helpful both for the proclamation of the readings, and for the preparation of the homily and the Prayer of the Faithful. It also provides a regular setting where ministers can assist one another - if a minister is reading too quietly, or too quickly, for example.

Of major importance for all ministers of the Word is how they participate in this liturgy when they are not directly involved as ministers. How we listen, and how we know our need to listen, and how we respond to what we hear, and how we know our need to respond to what we hear, will have a direct impact on how we minister God's living Word, on how we make ourselves available for Christ to minister to his people through us.

The Church is clear:

> The Liturgy of the Word is to be celebrated in such a way as to favour meditation and so any kind of haste such as hinders recollection is clearly to be avoided. In the course of it, brief periods of silence are also appropriate, accommodated to the assembled congregation; by means of these, under the action of the Holy Spirit, the Word of God may be grasped by the heart and a response through prayer may be prepared. It may be appropriate to observe such periods of silence, for example, before the Liturgy of the Word itself begins, after the First and Second Reading, and lastly at the conclusion of the homily.
>
> *GIRM 56*

The minister needs to be careful to ensure that God's faithful people are provided with the Word that is food for eternal life, and have time and space to draw nourishment from that food.

Liturgy of the Eucharist

Nourished by the divine Word, God's faithful have a deeper hunger for the Eucharistic food and drink. The Liturgy of the Word prepares us for the Liturgy of the Eucharist. It

gives us fresh reason for thanksgiving, and a keener sense
of our dependence on the grace of God.

Communion Rite

The word of God is not forgotten when it comes to
the Communion Rite. The Church has consistently
encouraged the singing of psalms as the faithful process
to Communion. Antiphons and psalms are indicated in the
Missal and the *Graduale Simplex* and *Graduale Romanum*
for the Entrance and Communion Songs. A community
that is being helped by its ministers to develop a love for
the Scriptures will find these songs especially helpful.

Concluding Rites

Minsters need to know the power and importance of the
dismissal. When we know the dismissal is not just 'the end',
but a new sending out of disciples to continue the mission of
the Church, we will be encouraged to seek out the pastoral
implications of the Scriptures we read to those disciples, and
be more careful yet to help those implications be expressed
both by the way we read, and by the way that the Scriptures
heard at Mass feed the pastoral and catechetical life of
the parish.

The Scriptures proclaimed at Mass can be seen as
nourishment not only for during the Mass but as food we
take away with us, to continue listening to and praying
with in the days to come.

Other aspects of liturgy and catechesis related to the ministry of the word

Song

It was noted above how it is encouraged that psalms and antiphons be sung at the entrance and during Communion, in preference to hymns. Sometimes this may not be possible. If that is the case it is good to ensure that the songs sung are - as well as being appropriate to the action of the Mass, and the season - Scriptural. Many hymn and liturgical song books have Scriptural indexes which help identify compositions which draw on the scripture readings of the day, or the season. This way the song supports the reflection on Scripture, and vice versa.

Preparation for Mass

Ministers of the word will of course need to read and pray their readings before Mass, to discern their meaning and consider how best to proclaim them. However the wider congregation too might be encouraged to familiarise (re-familiarise?) itself with the Sunday readings before coming to Mass. Often the Scriptures are not easy to appropriate on first reading, even when well-proclaimed. Preparing to hear them over the days before Sunday helps to a more prayerful and receptive listening.[6]

Continuing reflection after Mass (Mystagogy)

Especially important for our being nourished by the word of God is developing the awareness that we do not exhaust the meaning of a passage at a first hearing. Even if we have prayed with a passage before hearing it at Mass, returning to it again afterwards is a great help to our deeper hearing and response to what God says to us. The principle of repetition is key to the prayer practice of *Lectio Divina*.[7] This way of prayer, of particular value for ministers of the word, is something that might be encouraged more broadly in the parish community. Again, a community that is learning to be better fed by the word will become a more receptive congregation. Good listeners are likely to encourage readers to become better readers.

Catechesis

In the model homily for the institution of Lectors (the ministry of the word normally substituted for by commissioned Readers) the bishop says:

> Jesus Christ…entrusted his Church with the mission of preaching the Gospel to the whole world.
>
> As readers and bearers of God's word, you will assist in this mission, and so take on a special office within the Christian community; you will be given a responsibility in the service of the faith, which is rooted in the word of God. You will proclaim that word in the liturgical

assembly, instruct children and adults in the faith and prepare them to receive the sacraments worthily. You will bring the message of salvation to those who have not yet received it. Thus with your help men and women will come to know God our Father and his Son Jesus Christ, whom he sent, and so be able to reach eternal life.

Rite of Institution of Lectors, 4

Commissioned Readers do not have formal office in the Church. However by virtue of their familiarity with Scripture and their experience of ministering the word at liturgy they will often be in a good position to be part of the parish's catechetical team. They may not only assist with people's preparation for the sacraments but also support their community's participation in the new evangelisation[8], helping those already members of the Church to know and live their faith more fully, and help spread the good news still further beyond the obvious bounds of their community.

Other times of liturgy and prayer

Again the skills developed by a Reader at Mass will often make them suitable people for assisting and even leading other times of prayer and worship - for example the Liturgy of the Hours, or Liturgies of the Word when Mass cannot be celebrated.[9]

Guidelines for Ministers of the Word at Mass, leaders of Liturgy of the Word with Children and leaders of Liturgy of the Word and *Lectio Divina*

Training

It is necessary that those who exercise the ministry of Reader, even if they have not received institution, be truly qualified and carefully prepared so that the faithful may develop a warm and living love for Scripture from listening to the sacred texts read.

Their preparation must above all be spiritual, but what may be called a technical preparation is also needed. The spiritual preparation presupposes at least a biblical and liturgical formation. The purpose of their biblical formation is to give readers the ability to understand the readings in context and to perceive by the light of faith the central point of the revealed message. The liturgical formation ought to equip the readers to have some grasp of the meaning and structure of the liturgy of the Word and of the significance of its connection with the liturgy of the Eucharist. The technical preparation should make the readers more skilled in the art of reading publicly, either with the power of their own voice or with the help of sound equipment.

General Introduction to the Lectionary, 55

For the benefit of those whom readers are called to serve, the Church expects Readers to have the necessary skills to fulfil their role.

The bullet points below suggest a syllabus for formation of Readers. It is helpful for parishes to consider offering regular formation opportunities both for new and potential Ministers of the Word, and for all who are presently serving as Ministers of the Word. These should address the more basic needs of newer Ministers as well as enriching the skills and understanding of more established Ministers

Biblical Formation

- Introduction to Church's teaching of Revelation in sacred Scripture and Tradition
- Introduction to the Bible
- Relationship between the Old and New Testaments
- Introduction to key books and authors
- St Paul and his writings
- The Acts of the Apostles
- The other epistles and the book of Revelation
- The five books of the Torah: Genesis; Exodus; Leviticus; Numbers; Deuteronomy
- The Historical Books: e.g. Joshua, 1 & 2 Samuel and 1 & 2 Kings
- The Prophets: e.g. Isaiah, Jeremiah and Ezekiel

- The Psalms
- The other books: e.g. Wisdom, Ecclesiasticus, Daniel

Clearly it is important that readers have a proper appreciation of the Gospels, but these are not texts they proclaim so teaching about the Gospels is best offered in the context of teaching about the other books.

Liturgical Formation

- Introduction to the Lectionary
- The Liturgical Year and the Lectionary

Training in Public reading/speaking

- Voice production
- Presiding skills
- Cantor training (to assist in leading the singing of the Psalm and Gospel Acclamation)

Practical Guidance for ministers at Mass

Preparation beforehand

The minister will be advised which reading(s) they are to proclaim.

He/she will need to pray with the reading, considering its meaning in itself and, to the extent they can, its meaning in the canon of Scripture and the life of the Church and the local community. They will also need to think about the public reading of the passage: its tone and pace, the pronunciation of biblical names etc.

Newer readers might ask more experienced readers to help them practise reading it out loud, ideally in the church itself.

Arriving on time

Ministers work as members of a team, and it is an act of courtesy to the team, as well as the wider congregation to make sure they arrive in good time for the celebration of the Liturgy.

It is good practice to have a method of 'signing-in', and also an agreed time by which all ministers will have either signed in or been replaced by another minister.

On arrival the minister will check that the microphone is switched on; that the right volume of the Lectionary is ready and open at the right page for the first reading; that it is clear to all in the ministry team who is reading/singing what. The appropriate minister will also carefully review the text of the Biddings in the Prayer of the Faithful and, if they are to read them to the congregation, any Notices to be given at the end of the Mass.

Prayerful preparation

In the final minutes before Mass begins ministers might find it helpful to review the text they are to read.

The ministry team may also assemble in the sacristy to pray with the priest before Mass begins, and to form part of the entrance procession.

It may be helpful to note the order of ministers in the entrance procession:

- the thurifer carrying a smoking thurible, if incense is being used

- servers who carry lighted candles, and between them a server carrying the processional cross

- others ministers (e.g. servers, readers, cantors and commissioned ministers of Holy Communion)

- a reader carrying a Book of the Gospels, slightly elevated;

- the Priest who is to celebrate the Mass.

Those ministers who are not to be seated on the sanctuary will genuflect at entrance to the sanctuary (if the Blessed Sacrament is reserved there) and then make their way to their place. If the Blessed Sacrament is not reserved on the sanctuary, they will simply bow to the altar before making their way to their place.

Entering and leaving the sanctuary during Mass

Locally agreed practice will be observed as to what Ministers of the Word should wear when ministering (the basic choices are modest street clothing or an alb); whether all ministers come to and leave the sanctuary at the same time, or not; where to stand if not proceeding immediately to the ambo. Even if the Blessed Sacrament is reserved in the sanctuary ministers should not genuflect on entering/leaving the sanctuary: rather the minister should bow to the altar.

Proclaiming the word of God

Readers should wait for stillness in the congregation before announcing the reading: 'A reading from…'; pause before beginning the reading itself; and pause again before the concluding dialogue 'The word of the Lord: Thanks be to God.'

Leading the Prayer of the Faithful

The Biddings should be read by the deacon, if one is present. Alternatively they may be read by a lay minister of the word, or another pastoral minister.

In all cases the minister reads the invitation to prayer (e.g. 'Let us pray that…'). The prayer itself is offered by the congregation as it responds to the invitation. The minister reading the Biddings should therefore allow at least a period of ten seconds (count it! silently!) before the responsory, e.g. 'Lord in your mercy: Hear our prayer.'

Notices

If notices are to be read by a lay minister at the end of the Mass they should not be read from the Ambo, which is reserved for the ministry of the Word.

Leading Liturgy of the Word with Children

Full details of this form of Liturgy, and guidelines for its celebration, can be found on the Bishops' Conference Liturgy Office website.[10]

As in all Liturgies of the Word the Liturgy is ministered by a team of ministers. Those who have regular experience of assisting at the Liturgy of the Word will generally have skills which will be helpful in this more specialised form of celebration.

Leading a Liturgy of the Word

On occasion a Liturgy of the Word may be offered in a community, perhaps because it is seen as more helpful than a celebration of Mass for the community as a whole, or as more ecumenically hospitable form of Liturgy, or because Mass cannot be celebrated.

The form of the Liturgy can be found in the Bishops' Conference resource *Celebrations of the Word and Communion*.[11] The section 'Liturgy of Communion' should be omitted unless its use is authorised by the diocesan Bishop.

Again, this form of Liturgy is ministered by a team of ministers. Those who have regular experience of assisting at the Liturgy of the Word at Mass will generally have skills which will be helpful in this more specialised form of celebration.

Leading a time of *Lectio Divina*

Opening prayer

Use the Collect of the Sunday or the Day, adapting it for this new setting if necessary

Or the introduction from the Divine Office:

O God, come to our aid.

O Lord, make haste to help us.

Glory be to the Father and to the Son
and to the Holy Spirit,

as it was in the beginning, is now, and ever shall be,
world without end.

Amen. (Alleluia).

Or the phrase *'O that today we may listen to your voice, harden not our hearts'*

Spend a moment in silence after the prayer, continuing to pray to be open to the presence of God in the sacred Scriptures.

The reading

The chosen reading is read twice, ideally by different people, with an agreed time of silence (two or three minutes) between and after the reading. If a printed copy of the reading has been distributed, invite those present to put their sheet aside during this stage and listen, not read.

Before the readings take place suggest to people that they might like to listen for a particular word or phrase that might strike them, and if so use the word or phrase as a mantra during the time of silent prayer.

First sharing

After the second reading of the passage invite those present to share any particular word or phrase that struck them.

Silence

After the sharing observe another time of silence (two or three minutes)

Second sharing

Invite those present to share their thoughts or reflections on the reading. Ensure that participants listen to one another, and that sharing does not turn into discussion. This is a time for prayerful listening and not scholarly exegesis or debate. Gently encourage all present to participate in the sharing.

Ending the time of Lectio

You might invite participants to a time of spontaneous and intercessory prayer arising from the session.

Alternatively conclude the session with the Lord's Prayer or the Glory Be, or another prayer familiar to the all the participants. Also you can reflect on these questions:

- What in this chapter affirms good practice in your parish?

- What raises questions about the way ministers of the word are presently prepared for their ministry, or exercise it?

- What might be done to promote a deeper love and reverence for the Scriptures at Mass, and in the devotional life of the parish?

Order for the Blessing of Readers[12]

Introduction

1827 The word of God, as proclaimed in the sacred Scripture, lies at the heart of our Christian life and is integral to all our liturgical celebrations.

1828 This order is not intended for the institution of lectors by the bishop, who uses the rite contained in the Roman Pontifical. Rather, this blessing is for parish readers who have the responsibility of proclaiming the Scriptures at Mass and other liturgical services. Care should be taken to see that readers are properly prepared for the exercise of their ministry before receiving this blessing. The functions of the reader are given in no. 101 of the *General Instruction of the Roman Missal.*

1829 If desired, each new reader may be presented with a lectionary or bible after the prayer of blessing.

1830 This blessing is given by the pastor, who may also delegate it to another priest or a deacon.

Order of Blessing within Mass

1831 After the Gospel reading, the celebrant in the homily, based on the sacred text and pertinent to the

particular place and the people involved, explains
the meaning of the celebration.

General Intercessions

1832 The general intercessions follow, either in the
      form usual at Mass or in the form provided here.
      The celebrant concludes the intercessions with the
      prayer of blessing. From the following intentions
      those best for the occasion may be used or adapted,
      or other intentions that apply to the particular
      circumstances may be composed.

      The celebrant says:

      The word of God calls us out of darkness into the
      light of faith.

      With the confidence of God's children

      let us ask the Lord to hear our prayers and to bless
      these readers.

      R. Lord, hear our prayer.

      or

      R. Lord, graciously hear us.

      Assisting minister

      For the Church, that we may continue to respond to
      the Word of God which is proclaimed in our midst,
      we pray to the Lord.

For all who listen as the Scriptures are proclaimed, that God's word may find in them a fruitful field, we pray to the Lord.

For those who have not heard the message of Christ, that we may be willing to bring them the good news of salvation, we pray to the Lord.

For our readers, that with deep faith and confident voice they may announce God's saving word, we pray to the Lord.

Prayer of Blessing

1833   *With hands extended over the new readers the celebrant says immediately*:

Everlasting God,
when he read in the synagogue at Nazareth,
your Son proclaimed
the good news of salvation
for which he would give up his life.
Bless these readers.
As they proclaim your words of life,
strengthen their faith
that they may read with conviction
and boldness,
and put into practice what they read.
We ask this through Christ our Lord.
R. Amen.

Additional resources to support the Ministry of the Word

Bibles

The translation used at Mass in England and Wales is The Jerusalem Bible translation. The most helpful current edition is the Standard edition published by CTS with new notes by Henry Wansbrough, OSB.

For other translations in editions which provide fuller notes the following are recommended

The New Jerusalem Bible (standard edition) London: Darton Longman and Todd, 1985.

English Standard Version: *Study Bible*. Wheaton, Ill, USA, Crossway, 2008. *http://www.esvbible.org*

People's edition of Missal/Lectionary

CTS New Sunday Missal: *People's Edition with New Translation of the Mass*.

CTS New Daily Missal: *People's Edition with New Translation of the Mass* (with readings and Mass texts for Weekdays and Sundays).

Universalis - an on-line Missal and Divine Office using the translations approved for use in England and Wales, allowing you access to these books when using Android (including Kindle Fire), iOS (iPhone, iPad and iPod Touch), Mac and Windows. *www.universalis.com*

General

On the Mass

Pope St John Paul II (2003) *Ecclesia de Eucharistia*. London, Catholic Truth Society.

Pope St John Paul II (2004) *Mane Nobiscum Domine*. London, Catholic Truth Society.

Pope Benedict XVI (2007) *Sacramentum Caritatis*. London, Catholic Truth Society.

Pope Benedict XVI (2010) *Verbum Domini*. London, Catholic Truth Society.

Catholic Bishops' Conferences of England & Wales, Ireland, and Scotland. (1998) *One Bread One Body*. London, Catholic Truth Society.

Catholic Bishops' Conference of England & Wales. (2005) *Celebrating the Mass*. London, Catholic Truth Society.

Congregation for Divine Worship and Discipline of the Sacraments (2010). *General Instruction of the Roman Missal*, 3rd Typical Edition. London, Catholic Truth Society.

J. D. Crichton (1982) *Christian Celebration: Understanding the Mass*. London, Geoffrey Chapman.

Johannes H. Emminghaus (1978): *The Eucharist: Essence, Form, Celebration*. Collegeville, Liturgical Press.

Theological-Historical Commission for the Great Jubilee of the Year 2000 (1999). *Eucharist, Gift of Divine Life*. New York, Crossroad Publishing Co.

International Committee on English in the Liturgy (2010). *Become One Body One Spirit* (Interactive DVD). Washington, USA, ICEL.

Kevin W. Irwin (2005) *Models of the Eucharist*. Mahwah, NJ, Paulist Press.

Jerome Kodell (1998)*The Eucharist in the New Testament*. Collegeville, Michael Glazier Inc.

Peter M. J. Stravinskas (2000) *The Bible and the Mass*. Mt Pocono, PA, Newman House Press.

Paul Turner (2011) *At the Supper of the Lamb: A Pastoral and Theological Commentary on the Mass*. Chicago, Liturgical Training Publications.

On Scripture

Pope Benedict XVI (2010) *Verbum Domini*. London, Catholic Truth Society.

Catholic Bishops' Conferences of England and Wales and Scotland (2005) *The Gift of Scripture*. London. Catholic Truth Society.

Brown, Raymond E.(1985) *The Churches the Apostles left behind*. NY, Paulist Press.

Charpentier, E. (1982) *How to Read the Old Testament.* London, SCM Press.

Charpentier, E. (1982) *How to Read the New Testament.* London, SCM Press.

Pilch, John J (1996-2004) Three series, each of three books, one for each Sunday cycle of the Lectionary. *The Cultural World of the Prophets; The Cultural World of the Apostles*; *The Cultural World of Jesus.* Collegeville, Liturgical Press.

Pope Benedict XVI (Ratzinger, J.) (2007) *Jesus of Nazareth.* (3 volumes: *From the Baptism in the Jordan to the Transfiguration; Holy Week: from the Entrance into Jerusalem to the Resurrection; The Infancy Narratives*). London, Bloomsbury; Catholic Truth Society.

Reference

New Jerome Biblical Commentary (1995) London, Geoffrey Chapman.

More specialised

Pontifical Biblical Commission. (1993) *The Interpretation of the Bible in the Church. http://www.ewtn.com/library/curia/pbcinter.htm*

Pontifical Biblical Commission. (2001) *The Jewish People and Their Sacred Scriptures in the Christian Bible http://www.vatican.va/roman_curia/congregations/cfaith/pcb_documents/rc_con_cfaith_doc_20020212_popolo-ebraico_en.html*

Endnotes

[1] The principal guidance with regard to the celebration of Mass is published in the *General Instruction of the Roman Missal* (hereafter GIRM), the introduction to the *Roman Missal* and conveniently published as a separate volume by the Catholic Truth Society (RM12).

[2] In practice Bishops have chosen to confer these lay ministries of acolyte and lector only on for those preparing for ordination, as they are only permitted to be conferred on men. The Bishops have wished to see the ministry of proclaiming the readings from sacred Scripture open equally to both women and men and so have commissioned - deputed - them to this ministry as 'Readers' instead. The same is true where there is need for lay ministers to assist with the distribution of Holy Communion: the Bishops have authorised both women and men to be commissioned as (Extraordinary) ministers of Holy Communion.

[3] GIRM 91-109

[4] *http://www.liturgyoffice.org.uk/Calendar/Cycle/Index.shtml*

[5] It translates the Greek word ανάμνησις (anamnesis)

[6] A number of resources exist to help congregations with this. Many Catholic schools and parishes now make use of the Wednesday Word to help children and their families deepen their love for scripture (cf *www.wednesdayword.org*). Westminster Diocese offers a daily blog which prepares for the Sunday and reflects back afterwards, focussing especially on the readings from Scripture (*livingeucharist.wordpress.com*).

[7] Some simple guidance on this way of prayer is given in the following chapter.

[8] As urged in by Pope Francis in *Evangelii Gaudium*.

[9] When authorised by the Bishop these may include the Celebrations of the Word and Communion authorised by the *Directory for Sunday Celebrations in the Absence of a Priest* (Rome 1988)

[10] *http://www.liturgyoffice.org.uk/SOS/LOWC.pdf*

[11] h*ttp://www.liturgyoffice.org.uk/Resources/CWC/index.shtm*l

[12] This Rite comes from the *Book of Blessings* produced for use in the Dioceses of the United States. It is authorised by the Bishops' Conference for England and Wales for interim use in England and Wales.